To:
Patricia McNeish
& family

Sincerely

Margaret Gill
(Peggy)

# EVERYBODY LOVES DEBBIE

## by Margaret Bernice Gill

### Illustrated by
### Annette Packard Peck

**VANTAGE PRESS**
New York / Los Angeles / Chicago

*The royalties from this book have been donated to Saint Jude Children's Research Hospital, Memphis, Tennessee.

FIRST EDITION

All rights reserved, including the right of reproduction in whole or in part in any form.

Copyright © 1989 by Margaret Bernice Gill

Published by Vantage Press, Inc.
516 West 34th Street, New York, New York 10001

Manufactured in the United States of America
ISBN: 0-533-08580-2

Dedication:

To my dear grandchildren,
Stacey and David

Love, Grandma Gill

# Foreword

Before Debbie was adopted, boys and girls, her name was Fanola. She lived with my friend Agnes in Bayside, New York, for six years, from the time she was a young puppy. When my friend passed away, Fanola was left without a permanent home. I will now tell you the story of Fanola, how she came to be adopted by my husband and I and lived from then on in Wethersfield, Connecticut, where she was known as Debra Susan Gill, but we always called her our dear Debbie.

# Preface

If you have a dog or a special pet at home, I am sure you will always be kind to it. And, boys and girls, it will love you in return and be your friend.

Every night before I go to bed, my dog Debbie kneels close to me while I say my prayers, and this is the prayer I say.

"Dear Father in heaven, thank you for giving me Debbie. Please protect her every day and help her to grow strong. And, dear Father in heaven, please help all children who have pets be kind to them and love them as I love Debbie."

# EVERYBODY LOVES DEBBIE

It was a beautiful September day when my husband and I brought Fanola home with us from Bayside, New York. She had been living at the Sacred Heart Convent, also in Bayside, New York, after my friend, Agnes passed away. One of the sisters at the convent was also a friend to Agnes, and Sister did want to find a home for the dog. I knew this after speaking with Sister Kathleen on the telephone.

A few days later Frank (my husband) and I decided to visit Sister at the convent and ask her if she was going to keep Fanola permanently.

"I cannot," was Sister Kathleen's reply, "although we all love her here at the convent. But Sister Superior has told me that if I keep Fanola, it will not be fair to the other sisters at the convent because they might also like to have their own special pet."

When my husband and I went to Bayside a few days later, boys and girls, I just fell in love with the dog. Fanola knew both Mr. Gill and me because when we had gone for visits to see my friend Agnes in Bayside, which we did for many years, the dog would always greet us at the door. Sometimes she would give us her right paw to let us know she was happy to see us.

"Frank and I have talked about adopting Fanola," I said to Sister Kathleen. "We would like to have her for our own pet. As you know, Sister, we also have three cats at home in Connecticut, but Fanola will learn to play with them and accept them."

"Oh, that is just great," said Sister Kathleen. "The dog will be happy to have a family and live in the country after being in a New York suburb apartment for six years. As much as I and all the sisters at the convent will miss her, it is wonderful to know she will have a good home and be loved. That is what Agnes would have wanted for her.

"Before you leave, Mrs. Gill," added Sister Kathleen, "I must tell you that the young boy who lives next door to the convent always took Fanola for a walk every day after school. I am sure he would like to say good-bye to her before his classes begin this morning."

"Yes, Sister," I said, "that would be great."

So after the young boy gave Fanola a hug and Sister Kathleen wished us well, Mr. Gill put Fanola in the back seat of our car and I sat down next to her. "Say good-bye to your

friends now, Fanola," I said, "and off we will go to your new home in Wethersfield."

Fanola barked very loud, boys and girls, and as she put her head outside the car window, Sister Kathleen said, "God bless you all."

"Look, Sister," said the young boy, "she is like a little princess going away in her coach with her king and queen."

"And that she is," said Sister.

As soon as we arrived home in Wethersfield, Connecticut, Frank and I took Fanola all around the yard to show her where she could run and play every day and see all the buses go by on the street.

"Daddy will be taking you for long walks, dear Fanola," I said, "and you will meet other dogs going for long walks with someone in their family."

Then we took Fanola to meet Ginger Lattanzio, our neighbor's dog.

When Fanola entered our house, she got very quiet until suppertime. Then she saw me take out her two large bowls from the bag that Sister Kathleen had given me; one was for her water and the other for her food.

I prepared Fanola's supper and placed water in the other bowl. Fanola did not eat her dog food; she only drank the water. This went on for two days, until Frank and I decided to take Fanola to our veterinarian in Rocky Hill, Connecticut, where all our cats had been very well taken care of by Dr. David Havier and his staff at the animal hospital.

As soon as we opened the car door, Fanola flew out quickly. She started to tremble, because she somehow knew, boys and girls, that she was going to visit the doctor. You must always remember, boys and girls, that when your parents take you to visit your doctor, it is because they love you and want you to always be healthy.

"Good afternoon, Mr. and Mrs. Gill," said Dr. Havier. "Well, what have we here? It looks like you have added to your animal family."

"Yes, that is correct, doctor," I said. "The dog is now six years old, and she is a cocker-X. Can she be one of your patients?"

"I'd be delighted," said Dr. Havier, "but let me have her history. Then I'll take her in the next room and examine her.

"Now, Mrs. Gill, what is the dog's name?"

"She was named Fanola by her owner, Doctor, who passed away recently, but we have decided to change her name to Debra Susan Gill and call her Debbie."

Dr. Havier said to Debbie, "Let's shake hands and be friends, that's a big girl. You are doing fine. Now, let's see if you know your new name. Debbie 'jump up'."

Debbie barked as if to say, "I am going to like my new name, Debbie, and my adopted mommy and daddy."

"This is very important, Mrs. Gill," Dr. Havier told me. "Debbie will have to have more exercise. She must walk daily because she has too much weight on at present. Do not overfeed her.

"After completing my examination," Dr. Havier added, "I found the dog has a heart condition. I will give you medication that she must take every day in her food. And another thing, she must see me every six months for a check-up. Also, always give her plenty of water.

"Now, Debbie," Dr. Havier said, "I will give you your shots, then you can go back in the car and take a ride with your mommy and daddy to get your new license. Afterward, you will go back home where, I know, you will be given good care and, most of all, love."

Three months passed, boys and girls, and if only you could have seen Debbie. What a happy dog she was. She loved her mommy and daddy and her new home, where she had her own special room with all her toys. Every night she would place her toys near her rug. She always watched them very carefully, so no one would touch them.

In the morning while I would be reading the daily paper, the *Hartford Courant*, Debbie would try to reach the Kleenex in the back pocket of my robe. She would tear this into many pieces, then she would look up at me so proud of what she had done.

I would always praise her and say, "Oh, Debbie, what a big girl you are," even though I had to pick up all the pieces on the rug.

I always did forgive her. Why? Because I loved her, and that was her animal way of playing.

Debbie had great fun playing outdoors, and after breakfast, her daddy would take her for a walk. They always arrived back home before the mailman came.

Debbie loved John Orsino, our mailman, and every day she looked forward to seeing John. As she grew older, Debbie would stay near the front door and wait for John to bring the mail. When she saw him she would start to bark; then I would know she was happy and that John was coming.

"Well, well," John would say, "what do I have for my best girl today? Maybe a surprise in my left pocket." And dear Debbie knew it.

John would give Debbie the mail which she then brought to me. She was proud of that.

When Christmas came each year, John would give Debbie a gift to be put under the tree. One day he said to me, "Mrs. Gill, Debbie is a sweetie."

"Yes, she is, John," I said, "and everybody just loves her. I do hope we have her a long time."

When David and Stacey came to visit Grandma Gill, they always heard Debbie barking at the door and they could run into her room and talk to her. Debbie tried to tell them, in her own way, "I am so happy you came to visit with me. Come and see my toys and my nice room."

"Please, David," I would say, "just pet Debbie, but do not try to get close to her because she might think you are going to take her toy ball that she likes so much. She likes her toys and wants to protect them."

"We just like to come and see the dog," said Stacey. "She was so small when she came

to live here, but now she is a big dog. She is very friendly, Grandma."

What a wonderful pet Debbie was, boys and girls, and she knew all her friends and welcomed them whenever they came to visit with her at her house.

After having surgery, my mother came to stay with us in Wethersfield until she recovered. As soon as Debbie saw Nanny coming into the house, she rushed into her bedroom and kept very close to all her toys in the basket next to her bed. She started to bark very loudly at Nanny. She wanted to tell her not to take her toys away.

"Goodness, Debbie," said Nanny, "why are you so very upset? You know Nanny."

"It's because she knows you will be in the same bedroom with her, and that is her special place. She does not want anything changed," I said.

And Nanny said, "Give me your paw, Debbie. We are going to be good friends."

And Debbie gave Nanny a kiss and tried to tell her that she was happy and they were going to have fun.

Debbie made a lot of friends when she came to live in Wethersfield. One day Frank and I took her for a ride and stopped to see

our friend Jenny De Rosa, who is also an animal lover.

"Let's show Debbie to Jenny," I said to Frank. "I've told her all about the dog."

When we arrived at Jenny's doorstep, Debbie came tumbling out of the backseat of our car to see Jenny.

"What a beautiful girl you are," said Jenny. "I heard that you are a very good girl."

"She is, Jenny," I said. "And she's a great companion. It seems like she is always with me day and night."

"Someday when you and Frank go to New York or to visit with your mom, bring Debbie to spend the day with me. I would just love having her. She is a darling," said Jenny.

And so many times Debbie went to visit with Aunt Jenny. They became wonderful friends and pals together.

Ted Lewis, our cat, and Debbie played very well together, but Bonnie, our other small female cat, always tried to fight with Debbie. Sometimes, boys and girls, Ted Lewis would lift up his right paw and try to kiss Debbie, but Bonnie never tried to be friendly with other animals.

Bonnie would go into the woods in back of our house and stay in the bushes when it was warm. During the winter Bonnie just found a comfortable hiding place and slept most of the day. In fact, boys and girls, sometimes we had to look for Bonnie to come for her meals because she was always alone.

One spring day my friend Jane La Valley came for a visit with her dog. As soon as Jane entered the house, Debbie ran to her and barked very loudly over and over.

"Come, come, now, Debbie, you know Aunt Jane."

"Oh, Peggy," said Jane, "I think she knows I have my dog in the car. She probably wants me to take her for a ride. Now, Debbie, stop barking. You come and stay near me while I visit with your mom."

Soon the dog stopped barking and stayed close to her Aunt Jane.

"She is a wonderful dog," said Jane. "I know she is happy with you and Frank. She has a good home. I am sure that your friend Agnes would be delighted about that."

The seven years we had Debbie were all very happy years. Whenever we came home from church or shopping, she would always be at the door to welcome us. And sometimes,

boys and girls, she would jump up and try to kiss us to let us know how happy she was that we were back home with her.

It just seems that Debbie was with us in every room day or night. If Frank and I went into the living room to play the records, she was with us, or whenever I worked in the kitchen she was always close by watching me do the dishes or preparing dinner.

One day I said to Frank, "It's just great that we have Debbie with us all the time at home. Sometimes I wonder what we missed when we did not have her, but now she is our girl and we love her very much." And, boys and girls, Debbie knew that we loved her, too.

Boys and girls, I am sure you always enjoy taking vacations with your family and pets. Perhaps you visit with your grandparents, who love you so and give you gifts that make you happy.

One day Frank and I decided to take a trip to Los Angeles, California, after receiving an invitation from Rosemarie and Danny Thomas to attend the twenty-fifth anniversary of Saint Jude Children's Research Hospital. Later I asked, "What about Debbie? We can't take her on the plane to California with us."

"What about Aunt Jenny?" asked Frank. "I am sure Jenny and Ralph would be happy to have Debbie stay with them for five days."

And so off we went to California, boys and girls, and Debbie also had a wonderful stay with Aunt Jenny and Uncle Ralph.

When we returned from our trip, Debbie was delighted to see us again. She also had fun on her short vacation. But as soon as she came back home with us, she looked to see if all her toys were where she had left them, and they were, boys and girls.

One day I noticed that Debbie was not as playful as usual and that she was sleeping more than she usually did during the day. I even found her hiding under the bed in her room.

I called to her, "Debbie, come and see me," but she did not reply. When it was time for her supper, she pushed her dish away and only took her water.

*She must be sick*, I thought.

The next day Mr. Gill and I took Debbie to see Dr. Havier at the animal hospital. After he had examined her, he said, "I think it best that I keep her here overnight and do some tests on her. I also want to take an X ray because I suspect it could be her heart. She has been doing well for two years on her medication, but, Mrs. Gill, she is thirteen years old and her age is against her."

At that time I felt a great sadness within myself. As we left Debbie at the animal hospital, I gave her a kiss and hoped she would return home with us very soon.

Within a few days, boys and girls, Debbie was discharged from the animal hospital. We were so happy to bring her home with us again. Dr. Havier gave Mr. Gill and me all the results of her tests and informed us that she must now have only one-half can of her food daily and her water. I was to continue with her medication for her heart, but I had to increase the amount I put in her food every day.

"She must lose weight," said Dr. Havier. "It will be better for her heart. Please do not give her any treats until she has lost a few pounds. If at any time you notice Debbie is coughing, please call me at the office and bring her in, because it could be important."

Debbie slowed down her activities during the next six months, but she did continue with her meals and medication. One night as

I awoke I heard Debbie starting to cough as if she had something in her throat and could not get it out. She appeared to be uncomfortable.

During the morning Debbie continued coughing several times, she did not want to go outside with her daddy or take her water. Then she disappeared under the bed.

"I am afraid the time has come," I said to Frank.

"You get her ready," her daddy said, "and we will take her to the animal hospital."

And that we did, boys and girls.

Before leaving our house I called Aunt Jenny and asked her if she wanted to come see Debbie before we took her to the hospital.

"Of course," said Jenny. "I will be there in a few minutes."

As soon as Jenny had seen Debbie, she helped Frank place her in the car. With great sadness she said, "I am afraid that things do not look good for Debbie."

She gave Debbie a kiss and said, "I will always love you, Debbie. Try to be brave, Peggy," she added.

That same evening at nine o'clock Debbie passed away at the animal hospital in Rocky Hill, Connecticut. Dr. Havier later told us that she died very peacefully in her sleep. She had been kept comfortable to the end with oxygen treatment.

Debbie now sleeps in her final resting place with other animals at the Forest Rest Memorial Park in Glastonbury, Connecticut.

We are very sad that Debbie could not have stayed with us for more than seven years, but we will always remember the joy and devotion she gave to us and to all her friends who knew her in those years.

Our home is still very silent without Debbie, but the memories that she gave us and the happy times we had with her will always be remembered.

At Forest Rest Memorial Park Debbie's name is inscribed on her special monument. It reads:

Dear Debbie, and that is what she was to us, a very dear and devoted animal.